Crystalline Veils of Morning

A dance of lace in chilly light,
The cat skids by in a playful fright.
Outside the world wears a glittering gown,
While I sip cocoa in my fluffy brown.

Shivers of a Silent Night

The world's a snooze, yet I'm wide awake,
Debating if hot soup will charm the ache.
I peek outside, it's a snowy shop,
My nose against the glass, what's that? A mop?

Glassy Patterns in Still Air

Drawn shapes swirl and spin so fine,
A masterpiece by chill, oh so divine!
My breath's a fog, a comic show,
As I play tag with winter's glow.

Wintry Breath on Cold Glass

Muffin tops turn to mountain peaks,
Winter's here with funny tweaks.
I'll catch a snowflake, maybe two,
And end up with a frozen shoe!

Etched Dreams in Icy Patterns

Tiny crystals dance and play,
Hiding secrets, come what may.
Sweaters shriek and socks conspire,
Beans for warmth ignite the fire.

Each morning brings a patterned show,
Puppies sniffing at the glow.
Tea spills over, cup in hand,
While outside, snowflakes make their stand.

When Silence Follows the Cold

In the hush, the snowflakes taunt,
Squirrels chatter, but they can't flaunt.
Two left feet with boots that slide,
A penguin walk I can't abide.

Icicles hang like dental tools,
My poor car, it just drools.
Did your nose just freeze in place?
No, it's just the winter's grace!

Glistening Veils of a Silent Night

Stars twinkle in a frosty veil,
While I make cocoa, not to fail.
Whiskers twitch in frozen air,
Cats plotting their grand winter fair.

Neighbors bundled, looking like ships,
With scarves wrapped round their frosty lips.
Laughter echoes, cheerfully loud,
While snowflakes turn us all to clouds.

Windows to a Shivering Soul

Peering out, the world seems mad,
Blankets piled, who knew they'd add?
Watching snowmen with carrot noses,
While my toes feel like frozen roses.

Each breath fogs up the glass so clear,
Giggling at things that disappear.
Winter's grip, a playful tease,
As we munch on cookies with such ease.

Slumbering Night Beneath the Chill

The night is frosty, oh so bright,
Made crazier by the cat's mad flight.
With whiskers twitching, tail on fire,
He thinks he's chasing a squirrel choir.

Under blankets, we snuggle tight,
While outside sparkles in the white light.
The warmth of here, the chill out there,
Who knew frozen air could be so rare!

Secrets Treasures in Icy Etchings

I spy a dragon, sleek and grand,
A unicorn, oh! Isn't life just planned?
Yet it's merely splashes of dew,
What a circus of shapes that's true!

The kids outside, with laughter loud,
Making angels in the snowy cloud.
Meanwhile, my coffee gets colder still,
Oh, the things we do for winter's thrill!

Ethereal Designs in the Glare

Each petal of ice has a tale to weave,
Like that time I tripped on a sleeve!
Sketches form life's silly mistakes,
As my shoe prints look like crawling snakes.

We laugh at the patterns that life creates,
From smiles to fumbles, it celebrates.
So here we sip hot cocoa, so divine,
Watching winter's show with a glass of wine!

A Chill Spread Across the Glass

Windows dressed in icy lace,
Sometimes I wish for a warmer place.
Yet here I am with chatter and cheer,
While neighbors build snowmen with beer!

The mornings bring a bubbly surprise,
As dogs tango, with snow in their eyes.
We'll gather in coats, scarves tied in a knot,
Laughing together, life's jolly lot!

Chilled Artistry in Transparent Frames

A dance of ice on glassy panes,
Where little creatures lose their brains.
They tried to build a frosty town,
But slid right off, and tumbled down.

Each breath a puff, a cloud so fine,
Like drawing with a frozen line.
A squirrel skates, a birdlet slips,
While giggling dew drops steal their scripts.

Hushed Reflections on a Frigid Surface

In silence, creatures make a shout,
Imitating each clumsy bout.
A snail in skates, looking so spry,
Slides by a penguin in a tie.

Whispers echo in chilly air,
As winter's jokes get doled out fair.
Each breath a joke, each sigh a pun,
Who knew the cold could be such fun?

A Tapestry Woven in Ice

Patterns twirl like dancers prance,
A merry troupe in frozen pants.
Each swirl a story of laugh and play,
Beneath a sky so gray and gay.

Little critters out on the frost,
Searching for snacks, but finding they're lost.
Snowflakes spiral like curly fries,
While chilly winds give frosty high-fives.

The Breath that Bridges Seasons

A breath escapes, like cotton candy,
To bridge the gap, both sweet and dandy.
The flowers chuckle, although they're froze,
As winter wears its fancy clothes.

Puddles giggle at the sun's bright face,
While time spins gently in this race.
I swear I saw a snowman grin,
As spring tried sneaking back again.

Murmurs Caught in Glassy Glistens

Whispers dance on chilled glass,
Laughter trapped in frosty sass.
A cat leaps, surprised at the sight,
As patterns swirl in goofy delight.

Snowflakes nod, a curious crew,
Polka-dots made by clumsy dew.
The world outside, a frozen grin,
As cheeky critters play within.

Liminal Spaces of the Cold

Through the pane, the critters prance,
Playing tag in winter's dance.
A squirrel winks with a cheeky flair,
As icebergs grow in the afternoon air.

Giggling shadows, frosty cheer,
Snowmen plotting the best career.
They'd roll away if they could fly,
And toss their hats to the passing sky.

Surrender to a Snowy Dawn

As dawn arrives, with a snowy sigh,
The sun peeks out, 'tis a playful lie.
A burrito of blankets, this cozy fun,
With giggles and grumbles, the day's begun.

The kettle steams, a rebel's call,
With a sprinkle of humor, we conquer all.
Mug in hand, we take a glance,
At winter's world, a circus trance.

Transcendent Patterns of Winter's Touch

Swirls and twirls in icy lace,
A secret code of winter's grace.
The trees wear jackets, three sizes too big,
While the clouds above unleash a gig.

Footprints form a comedic trail,
As snowmen giggle, their cheeks turn pale.
Each crystal glistens with a grin so bright,
In this frosty world, everything feels right.

Messages Scrawled by Winter's Hand

A jolly artist at play,
He scribbles on glass with no delay.
Chilly doodles in a tangled spree,
What secrets he holds, just wait and see!

Snowflakes giggle, they jump and jive,
Whirling around like bees in a hive.
Each swirl and twirl, a playful tease,
Let's warm our hearts, if you please!

A Glowy Presence in White Delight

The world is painted, a canvas so bright,
With sparkling glimmers that tickle the night.
Shining smiles from the icy art,
Chasing away every shiver and dart.

A twinkling dance on shutters they spin,
In silent riot, they cheekily grin.
Who knew the cold could be such a hoot?
Dressed up in white, oh what a cute route!

Enigmatic Lace in the Frigid Glow

Delicate patterns like lace take the stage,
Winter's handwriting, a frosty sage.
Each line got a story, a giggle to share,
Causing the sun to stop and stare.

A whimsical world of chilly design,
Where snowflakes gossip over glasses of wine.
With each lazy drip, they melt away,
Leaving behind tales of their frosty play.

Drying Tears of the Frozen Sky

The sky let out a chuckle, then a sneeze,
As icicles formed, dangling with ease.
Droplets burst forth like a laugh from the past,
Tickling the panes with a spurt and a blast.

Glistening gems that shiver and shake,
Reflecting the light, all in good wake.
On windows they slide, an amusing affair,
Winter's comedy show, catch if you dare!

A Symphony of Winter Stains

Oh, the chilly artist's brush,
Leaves its mark in a rush,
Doodles on glass, so fine and bright,
Makes me giggle in pure delight.

Little creatures, a snowy crew,
Drawing mustaches, oh so cute,
A reindeer, a penguin, all in play,
Who knew winter would jest this way?

Mittens lost in a chilly gale,
Turned into art by nature's trail,
With each swirl, a laugh could burst,
In this world, cold serves up the worst.

But with cocoa warm in hand,
I sip and laugh, isn't it grand?
Each view a canvas, so absurd,
Nature's jokes, I've surely heard.

Whispers in the Dim Light

In the quiet, whispers glide,
On glassy sheets, they take their ride,
Smudged faces play peek-a-boo,
As I chuckle at the chilly view.

Cats sit pondering, looking wise,
While snowflakes swirl with silly sighs,
They dance like clowns in the morning glare,
Who knew that snow could cause such flair?

The moonlight beams on icy lace,
Making every hiccup look like grace,
A frosty twirl in a wobbly line,
Makes me grin like I've drank a brine.

As I watch the night unfold,
Each giggle from the cold retold,
With every shiver that draws a laugh,
Winter's whimsy on this path.

Diamond Patterns of Frozen Grace

Beneath the icy stage they shine,
Little gems that playfully entwine,
Twinkling bright in the morning sun,
Each a joke, oh what fun!

I see squiggles of a snowman's hat,
Fluffy scarves and a snowdog's spat,
When the sun comes out, giggles ignite,
At this chilly show, all feels right.

Glittering on glass like a cheeky grin,
Making the mundane a whimsical spin,
A ballet of patterns, crisp and neat,
Nature's laugh in frosty beat.

With every pattern, a chuckle stirs,
Even those cold, unkind winters,
Bring on the humor, the fun, the cheer,
Under diamond skies, we persevere.

Touched by the Chill of the Heavens

Up in the sky, a frosty deep,
Silly clouds play hide and seep,
Sprinkling giggles, pure and bright,
A chilly touch turns wrong to right.

Kids outside, building with glee,
A snowman named Frosty, you see,
He wears a hat quite askew,
And a carrot nose with a view.

The chilly air brings laughs galore,
While snowball fights lead to uproar,
With every throw, a joyful squeal,
Winter's playtime is quite the deal.

When the night falls, the laughter swells,
Echoing through the frosty bells,
As we huddle close, the warmth we share,
In winter's grasp, there's joy everywhere.

Frosty Memories in Whispered Light

Tiny patterns dancing bright,
Each swirl a silly flight.
My breath fogs the glass so well,
Like a secret I can't tell.

Chilly ghosts with frozen grins,
Trace my day with icy pins.
They giggle as I slip and slide,
On this wintertime joyride.

Cats outside in coats of white,
Chasing snowflakes in delight.
While I sip my cocoa warm,
Hoping none will raise alarm.

Memories twirl like falling snow,
Each one makes my spirit glow.
Through winter's fun, I find retreat,
In laughter, cold can be so sweet.

The Art of Wintry Scribbles

Doodles formed with frosty breath,
Masterpieces until the death.
A heart-shaped blob, a silly fish,
An elephant who grants a wish.

My artistic skills are quite the sight,
In chill, they vanish, oh what a plight!
I curse the cold for stealing art,
But laughter warms this frosty heart.

Snowflakes twirling, fancy and fast,
They race to see who'll fall last.
With crayons made of frozen dreams,
I'll sketch the dance, or so it seems.

Outside, the world is a wonderland,
While I doodle with a frozen hand.
But giggles echo, fill the air,
Like my art, it's beyond compare.

An Ethereal Gaze through Icy Veils

Through crystal panes, I peer and see,
A world that's giggling just for me.
A penguin's ballet, quite absurd,
Slipping, sliding, oh how they stirred!

Snowmen wear hats, askew and bright,
Holding snowball fights in the night.
A mistletoe accident is near,
When the cat steals kisses—oh dear!

Mittens tossed in playful fits,
As chilly hands create small skits.
In laughter, warmth emerges strong,
Even in winter, can't go wrong!

Nature's canvas, a wink, a tease,
I can't help but laugh with ease.
In frosty air, the fun's alive,
With icy giggles, we all thrive!

Nature's Breath in Shimmering Silence

Tiny crystals claim the glass,
A chilly job, it seems, alas.
The cat has slipped, it starts to slide,
On sparkling tales, it tries to glide.

The plants are dressed in icy lace,
Each leaf a frozen, silly face.
They giggle when the sunlight peeks,
And start retelling winter freaks.

Pigeons puff their feathery chests,
As if their winter wardrobe's best.
They strut and dance with fluffed-up pride,
As chilly breezes swirl and glide.

Hats' tips are frozen, noses too,
Yet somehow, all is fun to do.
In nature's playful, frosty show,
The world's a giggle, don't you know?

A Canvas of Winter's Secrets

Painting whispers on the panes,
A hidden world that gently gains.
The trees are scribbling silly rhymes,
While squirrels plan their acorn crimes.

Snowflakes tumble in balletic grace,
They giggle, scatter, then embrace.
Each flake a painter in disguise,
Creating laughter 'neath gray skies.

The chilly wind, a stand-up act,
With every blow, a funny fact.
It swirls around with glee and cheer,
As children chase what disappears.

Even the shadows start to smile,
As frozen giggles stretch a mile.
A canvas bright, a frosty tease,
Nature's art, a jolly freeze!

Glacial Artifacts of Thought

Seeing your breath in puffy clouds,
We compete with the chill in crowds.
Whispers echo, laughter bright,
In the crisp air, we take our flight.

Hands so cold, my nose is red,
Frosty dreams bounce in my head.
Carrot noses line the street,
Snowmen laugh, they can't be beat.

The ground is slick, we wobble wide,
On frozen slips, a snowy ride.
Oops, I fall into a drift,
Winter's smile, the best of gifts.

The sun peeks out, it's warm and rude,
Burning off our silly mood.
But we'll share our frosty cheer,
With stories told to warm the year!

The Cool Caress of Morning Light

Morning breaks with nippy flair,
Sunshine glitters everywhere.
Sneakers squish on frosted grass,
As warm hopes spark with every pass.

Mittens dance on chilly hands,
In playful jingles, winter stands.
The rooftops wear a shiny hue,
As snowflakes laugh, they swirl anew.

Icicles dangle, tips so sweet,
Snowball fights can't be discrete.
Giggles echo through the park,
With every fling and playful spark.

As sunlight melts the chilly dawn,
We raise our scarves, the frost withdrawn.
In winter's laughter, there's delight,
Nature's fun beneath the light!

A Chill as Art on the Glass

Little swirls and twirls so neat,
They dance like penguins on the street.
A masterpiece I can't ignore,
Who knew my window could decor?

I grab my mug, I sip and stare,
My icy canvas beyond compare.
Coffee steaming, a warm delight,
While outside, frost puts up a fight.

A snowflake's waltz, a winter show,
Just outside, the world's aglow.
With every breath, the chill we freeze,
I laugh and think, 'Oh, winter, please!'

That artful chill, so curious,
Makes every morning quite glorious.
With silly shapes that beg a giggle,
I trace a bunny, then a wiggle.

The Story Told in Ice and Light

A crystal fable on my pane,
A dragon's tale, a frosty reign.
Little figures, quite absurd,
A penguin choir, how they're heard!

One little snowman, quite a clown,
Waving high from his chilly crown.
While icicles point with glee,
They seem to joke, 'Just wait and see.'

With every breath, I make a scene,
A frosty circus, sleek and keen.
The snowmen dance, the snowflakes cheer,
This chilly cast brings lots of cheer.

And as the sunlight takes a peek,
These winter tales are quite unique.
The window tells its funny lore,
Oh, winter's art, I do adore!

Glimmering Traces of the Cold

On my window, a shimmering haze,
Little sparkles in such funny ways.
The icy squiggles play a tune,
A chilly dance beneath the moon.

I sit and laugh at shapes I see,
A walrus laughing back at me!
A snowflake frowns, a chilly pout,
While snowmen giggle, skipping about.

Each breath a story, each sigh a line,
The chilly air is doing just fine.
With ghostly hands, it draws the night,
A fanciful world of pure delight.

So let the cold come, let it stay,
With laughter echoing in the fray.
These glimmers of ice, such joyful finds,
In winter's hold, it warms the minds.

Specks of Winter's Breath

Tiny jewels on my glass await,
A frozen tale that's sure to elate.
The winter's giggle, a chilly quirk,
As icy tendrils do their work.

Little creatures prance and sway,
In crystal lines, they come to play.
A squirrel in a hat, looking for cheer,
With fluffy snowflakes, oh so dear.

Each exhale puffs a giggly mist,
Creating shapes that twist and twist.
A polka-dotted snowman dancing near,
What a sight, it brings such cheer!

With every breath, the stories rise,
In frosty art, the laughter lies.
I raise my cup and toast the cold,
To winter's whimsy, bright and bold!

Reflections of an Icy Muse

In the morning chill, visions appear,
A frozen artist, sipping cheer.
Sketches of snowflakes dance and twirl,
Creating faces that giggle and whirl.

The coffee's hot, the laughter's bright,
As I trace giggles through the night.
With every sip, the patterns play,
As if the ice wants to say 'Hey!'

I doodle mustaches on the glass,
Each swirl a joke that none can pass.
A giggly prank on winter's sheet,
Shining lollipop in cold retreat.

So let us toast to chilly jest,
Where giggles play and ice is best.
In every glimmer, laughter's near,
A winter's jest, I hold so dear.

Celestial Frost and Shattered Light

Stars in the cold play peek-a-boo,
With frosty shimmers, a sparkling crew.
They wink and nod, glowing bright,
As I chase their trails with sheer delight.

The sunlight tickles the icy sheen,
Creating glimmers, a playful scene.
'Tis nature's disco, a grand show,
With every twinkle, spirits glow.

Of comets that slip and mistakes that shine,
The jovial dance is truly divine.
A laugh, a cheer, as skies collide,
With chilly sparks, our joy can't hide.

So here I stand, a witness to fun,
With chilly chuckles, I'm always spun.
For every shard, I see a joke,
In this frosty play, my laughter's woke.

Lacy Prints of Winter's Heart

Delicate patterns weave without care,
Whorls of laughter go everywhere.
An artist's hand in nature's sway,
Drawing giggles in a marbled play.

The chilly breath creates a game,
With each swirl, a snowflake name.
I find a smile in every line,
As if the cold has had some wine.

Translucent giggles smear and smear,
Each breath a chuckle, crisp and clear.
I make a face, it starts to melt,
Oh, winter's love, what fun you've dealt!

Beneath the icy, playful art,
Lies a winter's whimsical heart.
And though it's cold, let laughter burst,
In these lacy prints, joy's well rehearsed.

Tracing the Breath of the Night

When night descends, the laughter begins,
With whispers cold that tickle my skin.
I trace my breath, a foggy sign,
As the window giggles, feeling fine.

The moonlight plays with crunchy bits,
While shadows dance like little fits.
With every puff, a comic freeze,
A chilly wink puts me at ease.

The jokes are faint, but clear to see,
In every line, a chuckling spree.
A snowman grins with sparkly glee,
His carrot nose—oh, what a spree!

So here in the night, we share a riddle,
With breaths of joy, we laugh and twiddle.
In chilly moments, pure delight,
I'm tracing giggles in the night.

Serene Kisses of the Icy Dawn

Morning greets with chilly breath,
A dance of crystals, not of death.
My breath, a dragon, puffs and pouts,
While I dodge the cold, my face just shouts!

Windows wear their frosty dress,
Like a bride, in icy finesse.
I tap and laugh, a magic show,
As tiny flakes start to ebb and flow.

The sun peeks out, a cheeky grin,
Lenient at last, let the fun begin!
With tea in hand, I smile so bright,
But here comes cold, a playful bite!

Glorious chill, oh what a tease,
Life's frosty art, a winter breeze.
Around it all, my laughter chimes,
As mornings spin on merry rhymes.

Veils of Silver in the Blue

I wake to find the world adorned,
With veils of silver, winter's horn.
A canvas pure, yet wild and free,
Nature's giggle looks right at me!

Icicles hang like nature's fangs,
While snowflakes dance in playful gangs.
I trip and slide, a joyous mess,
"Call it art!" I proudly confess.

My coffee steams, a jiggle, a swirl,
I spill a drop, it's winter's whirl.
Hot chocolate dreams in marshmallow boats,
Life's frosty adventure, on igloos we float!

Through the window, the view's a jest,
Each crystal sparkles, wearing a vest.
So here I stand, a grinning fool,
In the icy school of winter's rule.

Ephemeral Artistry of the Freeze

The world outside looks like a dream,
Nature's canvas, a silvery gleam.
With every breath, a cloud appears,
I laugh aloud, while sipping beers!

Shivering trees, they sway and grin,
Playing hide and seek with wind's spin.
Every branch, a frosted crown,
Winter giggles when I fall down.

My nose is red, like Rudolph's tale,
And mittens slip, oh what a fail!
Snowmen cheer, adorned in scarves,
As I navigate this icy spars.

Frosty footprints, a silly track,
With each cold step, I can't hold back.
As winter paints with joy in mind,
Its artistry leaves funny behind.

Celestial Curves in Icy Stillness

A chilly morning, sky so grand,
I scribble on glass, it feels like sand.
A laugh escapes, as curves take flight,
My finger twirls in pure delight!

With every swirl, a frosty show,
Creating worlds where giggles grow.
Like a comedian's studio stage,
I draw a smile, unleash the sage!

The air is crisp, a sparkly bite,
This enchanting chill, a strange delight.
I pull my scarf, a cozy hug,
Winter's embrace, a friendly tug.

Amidst the cold, I find my cheer,
Surrounded by laughter, winter's near.
So let it snow, with joy I'll blend,
In icy stillness, fun has no end!

Shards of Light in a Winter Cloak

Sunbeams dance like clumsy elves,
Casting shadows, not themselves.
Snowmen laugh with carrot grins,
While penguins wear their woolly skins.

Icicles hang like pointy teeth,
Making each breath sound like a wreath.
Hot cocoa spills from tipsy mugs,
As marshmallows jump like little bugs.

Frosted patterns swirl and twine,
On glassy panes, a great design.
Squirrels chuckle, tails held high,
While clouds play hide and seek in the sky.

The world's a stage, a winter show,
With laughter echoing through the snow.
Each chilly breeze a giggle shared,
In this frosty realm, no one's scared.

Breathe the Chill of Forgotten Mornings

Chilly whispers creep through the air,
Noses sniffle, but who can care?
Under blankets, we hide and play,
While socks attempt to run away.

Frozen fingers, dashing outside,
Leap into snowballs with great pride.
But wait! What's this? A snowflake hat?
I can't tell if it's snow or a cat.

Mittens clash like rival teams,
As winter plays out crazy dreams.
A snowball duel in the front yard,
Ends up with one very soggy bard!

Mornings forgotten, a frosty tease,
As winter's chill brings silly grins,
In icy laughter, we'll find our way,
Through each brittle, funny winter day.

Lacy Whispers in the Stillness

Whispers of lace drape the night,
As snowflakes twirl in the pale moonlight.
Elves in mittens, cold at play,
Roll up snowballs, come what may!

Chattering teeth, a merry sight,
While penguins slide left and right.
A talking snowman with a hat,
Tells jokes to birds who giggle back!

Icicles shimmer, like done-up hair,
Nature styling, beyond compare.
Belly laughs echo down the lane,
As winter's chill is never plain.

Tiptoe through the frozen spry,
As giggly breezes whisper by.
Lacy dreams in cold delight,
Keep our hearts warm through the night.

The Poetry of a Frozen Veil

Hidden lines in the frozen mist,
Crafting stories that can't be missed.
Jokes that dance on icy air,
With every breath, a playful dare.

Sleds slip down the hills with glee,
As laughter echoes endlessly.
Snowflakes jest, they twirl and spin,
Daring kids to join the fun within!

In the stillness, giggles grow,
While winter whispers secrets low.
With every splash of chilly cheer,
We create a world where joy draws near.

So raise a mug, let laughter sail,
Celebrate the quirks in every trail.
For in this frozen, snowy land,
The heart finds warmth through hand in hand.

A Breath of Ice in the Starlit Dark

Chilly whispers float in the air,
Snowflakes giggle, caught unaware.
Sipping cocoa, warm and bright,
My teeth chatter, what a sight!

Mittens lost, they play hide and seek,
A snowman grins with a carrot beak.
Hot cocoa spills down my chin,
I take a sip, and the fun begins!

Slippery steps on the frozen ground,
I'm a penguin with grace, so profound.
My laughter rings, a silly tune,
As I slip and slide to the moon!

Under starlight, I dance and slip,
A frosty crown for my wobbly trip.
Laughter echoes in the night,
In this icy wonderland, what a delight!

Woven Silence of a Wintry Night

Under the quilt of night's embrace,
A snowball flies, strikes my face.
Chasing shadows, I lose my hat,
Frosty kisses, oh what of that?

Snowmen stand like tall, proud guards,
I throw a snowball, it hits the cards!
Laughter lingers in the chilled air,
As we tumble without a care.

Giggling through the icy maze,
Chasing each other in a frosty daze.
The world's aglow, a shiny white,
With every giggle, we take flight!

The night whispers secrets, so sweet,
While snowflakes dance at our little feet.
Woven dreams in cold delight,
Endless fun in wintry night!

Beauty Bound in Shimmering Sheets

A blanket of white wraps around tight,
Stars twinkle down with a cheeky light.
The air crisp, like a minty breath,
A snowman plots to cause my death!

With carrot noses and eyes of coal,
He grins with mischief, ready to roll.
I take a step, a slip, a slide,
Now my dignity, I must hide!

Icicles dangle like frozen teeth,
As snowballs launch, I shout beneath.
Who knew winter could be such fun?
Even when all my clothes come undone!

In laughter wrapped, we play and tease,
While shivering in a wintry breeze.
Beauty shines in this frosty scene,
A jolly jest, so serene!

Hushed Murmurs on the Glass

Tiny patterns bloom on the glass,
I doodle shapes as the moments pass.
Giggles echo, we're lost in cheer,
As snowflakes tickle, I shift my gear.

My boots crunch loud on the sparkling lane,
Slipping and sliding, oh what a gain!
Caught in a flurry of frosty delight,
We tumble and roll, oh what a sight!

Hushed giggles float as the night unfolds,
In each corner, a frosty tale told.
Winter's mischief, a comical play,
With laughter and freezes leading the way.

Wrapped in warmth and grinning wide,
We chase the chill, we'll never hide.
For in this magic of wintry sway,
Laughter and ice will always stay!

Frozen Whispers in the Twilight

Chilly whispers dance on glass,
As I sip my cocoa fast.
The cat, in boots, does prance around,
Wishing for warm and solid ground.

A snowman's hat flies in the breeze,
Twirling round with playful ease.
I swear at that and let out a shout,
Why's he the one that's getting about?

My breath makes ghosts that spook the night,
They giggle softly, what a sight!
Each puff a joke that floats away,
Leaving me laughing at the play.

So as the world turns crisp and bright,
I'll share my joy with all in sight.
For every chill has laughter baked,
In frozen lands, it can't be faked.

Shimmering Shadows of the Cold

The moonbeam winks through frozen lace,
While squirrels in coats begin to race.
Snowballs fly from every arm,
As giggles echo, causing charm.

A penguin slipped, and down it went,
Right into my snowman's dent!
It looked at me with puppy eyes,
As if to say, 'What a surprise!'

Down the street, the laughter blooms,
As snowmen gather like vacuum brooms.
They gossip, and they trade their hats,
While I dodge, the King of Cats.

In silver shadows, fun prevails,
Where icy tales weave winter trails.
We dance and spin, hearts so bold,
In shimmering realms of the cold.

Veiled Vignettes by the Hearth

Crisp air wraps around my toes,
As I laugh at silly woes.
The fire pops, a cozy tune,
While socks dance like a merry moon.

I tell a tale of icecream lanes,
Where drizzles freeze and cause such pains.
Each scoop a laugh, each cone a cheer,
As we slip and slide without fear.

The cat looks on with a raised brow,
"What's all this fuss? Pray, tell me how!"
And I burst out with tales so tall,
As splatter-patter's our winter ball.

By the hearth's glow, spirits unwind,
Frolicking fun in every kind.
Through stories, warmth, a winter's greet,
In veiled vignettes, life's a treat!

Traces of a Breathless Night

Underneath the twinkling stars,
Snowflakes scatter like tiny cars.
The wind comes in with a silly grin,
Tickling noses—let the fun begin!

My fingers dance like frosty sprites,
Sketching dreams on chilly nights.
Each breath a cloud that's brief and bold,
Painting giggles on pathways of cold.

A turtle on a sled is brave,
Sliding down with every wave.
I can't help but laugh at the sight,
As he tumbles in pure delight.

In the moon's glow, our joy ignites,
With traces of laughter in the nights.
We chase the chill, we run, we play,
In frosty realms where giggles sway.

Portraits in Ice and Light

A canvas of crystals, so sly and bright,
Little monsters tease on a chilly night.
Imagined faces, all frozen in time,
Smiling at us with a laugh and a rhyme.

I see a penguin in a top hat's grace,
Waving hello in this wintry embrace.
A cat in a scarf, looking quite debonair,
In this quirky gallery, joy fills the air.

Each cheeky character, a tale to unfold,
An icy comedian, mischievous and bold.
With every warm breath, they start to recline,
Vanishing slowly, it's their end of the line.

As laughter dissolves in the shimmering light,
They wink at my heart and take graceful flight.
These portraits of joy, trapped in a show,
Tell tales of the winter's magical glow.

Nature's Breath on the Surface

A breath from the sky lands with a giggle,
Painting the glass, it starts to wiggle.
Figures emerge, a bunny and pie,
A dance of delight under the morning sky.

The sun peeks in, with a tickle and tease,
I swear I just saw a polar bear sneeze!
He wears quite the hat, oh what a sight,
Giggling at nature's whimsical plight.

Clouds overhead, a popcorn machine,
Popping out laughter, a joyful routine.
Each little bubble, like whispers of fun,
Chasing away shadows, shining like sun.

With each little breath, it's a comedy show,
Nature's performance, it steals the glow.
A theater of chill, where chuckles flow free,
This painted laughter, my winter's jubilee.

Winter's Lullaby in Transparent Hues

In the hush of the night, a melody clear,
I hear frosted whispers that dance in my ear.
A choir of giggles, a serendipitous tune,
With sparkles of mischief that twirl 'neath the moon.

The trees wear jackets, their branches so spry,
Singing to snowflakes as they flutter by.
Each drop of ice with a quirky delight,
Echoes of laughter spread wide in the night.

An orchestra of jests, each note full of cheer,
The winter winds carry all we hold dear.
Jokes on the weather, it's all in good fun,
A symphony bright, under the glimmering sun.

So curl up, dear friend, let this lullaby rise,
With humor and warmth, it's a sweet surprise.
In this wondrous season, with giggles abound,
A whimsical winter, where joy can be found.

Ethereal Gardens of Jack's Touch

In a garden of wonders where frolics abide,
Whispers of nonsense dance side by side.
Tulips in socks, and daisies in hats,
All marching together like oddly cute brats.

The petunias giggle, their colors ablaze,
While snowflakes tease with their fluttering prance.
An ice cream tree, how absurd it may seem,
It chuckles and jiggles, like a whimsical dream.

In this realm of laughter, where cheer takes its flight,
Penguins play hopscotch 'neath a moonbeam light.
Each frosty creation, a jest in the cold,
An ethereal garden, with stories retold.

As snowmen attempt to dance in a row,
They tumble and giggle, a roguish tableau.
With each frosty twinkle, my heartbeats align,
In Jack's joyful garden, magic is divine.

Crystal Lace in Morning's Glow

Tiny jewels dance, catching the light,
A laugh in the morn, oh what a sight!
Shapes like snowflakes, odd and grand,
I sip my cocoa with frozen hand.

Chasing my cat who pounces and plays,
Unlocking the secrets of wintery gaze.
She leaps at the lace upon the glass,
Wonders if magic is there to amass.

Birds in a frenzy, they tap and they poke,
Wondering if windows are meant to be broke.
Each little bump, ringtone of cheer,
As I chuckle behind my hot cup of beer.

With a wink and a giggle, the day starts anew,
Each pattern a story, each peak a view.
Winter's a prankster, wearing a crown,
And I'm the jester, just floating around.

Silent Stories on a Shivering Pane

A thousand tales etched, like whispers of old,
Tiny ice gardens, their wonders unfold.
I stare at the shapes, I swear I can see,
An elephant dancing, just waving at me!

My morning toast pops, a toast to the day,
But the window mocks me, it's gone astray.
'The butter will melt!' I exclaim with a grin,
As the cat sees the ghost of a frozen old chin.

Sipping my tea, no worries in sight,
Suddenly shocked by a snowball in flight!
My neighbor's delight as I duck and I weave,
While the window keeps secrets that never believe.

Yes, winter is funny with frosty cheer,
Sketching out laughter, it's oh-so sincere.
Each breath on the glass, a giggle in sleep,
As I wonder what views tomorrow will keep.

A Tapestry of Winter's Breath

Threads of ice weave stories along the way,
Trying to catch me while I'm at play.
With a cup of warm joy, I gaze with delight,
At the silly shapes dancing, what a sight!

Bunnies in mittens, frolicking with style,
Chasing bright snowflakes, oh how they beguile.
But socks on the floor threaten chaos and gloom,
As icicles giggle, they jingle in bloom.

Vines of glitter brought in by the breeze,
Scribbling in patterns, winter's own tease.
A parade of shapes, the antics they bring,
As I chuckle and wonder, what's next in this fling?

Joked by the thaw, in warm laughter I bask,
With stories of whimsy, it's all I could ask.
Winter's a prankster, and oh how I cheer,
For each chilly moment, I'll hold ever dear.

Glacial Poems on Glass

Whispers of winter are wrapped up in lace,
Conversations of snowflakes in their frosty embrace.
Each curve and each twist a giggle or two,
As squirrels gather tales, and I join the queue.

With crayons and charcoal, I draw what I see,
A hat and a scarf on an old snowy tree.
But that sneaky puppy—what's he got to share?
As he catches the snowflakes all up in my hair!

Tickling the glass with a breath of delight,
A canvas of laughter from morning to night.
Giggles erupt as I swipe at the mist,
Each mark is a treasure, an icy humorist.

So here's to the chill, the chill that inspires,
A canvas of laughter that never tires.
With each icy puzzle, each chuckle I find,
I embrace the magic, all silly and kind.

The Elegance of a Glacial Glimpse

On chilly mornings, quite a sight,
Patterns dance in the morning light.
The glass is art, oh what a tease,
Who knew ice could play with such ease?

Tiny castles, tangled trees,
Admiring this art with a sneeze.
I giggle as I sip my brew,
My breath a cloud, a little zoo!

The dog barks at the glassy show,
While pigeons cock their heads down low.
With every swirl, my thoughts take flight,
Decorated windows, pure delight!

A masterpiece, a chilly prank,
Thanks, old man winter, full of spank!
I'll raise a toast, my drink in hand,
To this cool magic, oh so grand!

Memories Trapped in Crystal

Each window tells a story grand,
With icy scribbles made by hand.
A squiggly line, a wavy spiral,
All signs of winter's cheeky trial.

I see my mate, a funny goat,
Doing the cha-cha with a coat.
Filled with giggles, laughter sings,
As nature gives us frosted things.

We watch the flakes perform their dance,
Creatures prancing in a trance.
With nibbled snacks in cozy chairs,
Frozen chuckles fill the air.

The window glass, a funny frame,
Reflects our joys, the silly game.
This chilly charm, a wink for me,
In crystal tales, I'm wild and free!

Chill Whispered Dreams

Upon the glass, a chilly breeze,
Whispers secrets, ancient tease.
I watch the shapes morph and sway,
As midnight giggles drift away.

My dreams are caught in icy lace,
Painted patterns, a frozen place.
A snowman winks with carrot nose,
While frosty spirits play their prose.

Puddle jumpers, hooted swoon,
Dance beneath the silver moon.
With every breath, a cloud of cheer,
A winter party drawing near!

With laughter echoing through the night,
The chilly dreams, a joyous flight.
As morning comes, I bid adieu,
To frosty tales that always woo!

Icy Etchings of Dawn

As dawn is born, a glimmering treat,
The window leaves its chilly seat.
With every pearl, a chuckling cheer,
The world awakes, no hint of fear.

Beneath the sun, the sparkles play,
Like little sprites in bright ballet.
I watch in awe, a giggly gaze,
The glass parade, a frosted craze.

Sipping cocoa, in cozy bliss,
With rosy cheeks, I can't resist.
Each icy story, a funny twist,
I find a smile that can't be missed!

So here's to mornings, crisp and fine,
Where icy laughs and whims entwine.
My frosty friend, a gift divine,
A giggle wrapped in winter's line!

Dialogues with the Chilled Air

Oh dear chilly breath, you giggle so loud,
Whispering secrets beneath your soft shroud.
You dance on the glass, a mischievous sprite,
Playing hide and seek each day and each night.

I see you there, with your frosty array,
Drawing silly faces in your own icy way.
You tease with your sparkle, then vanish away,
Leaving me chuckling, come what may!

Your laughter echoes in the morning light,
Turning my snooze into a comedic fright.
"Get up!" you chime, "The day's cold yet bright!"
I roll over snickering, pondering your plight.

When mists of joy fill my tepid old room,
With every breath, you manage to bloom.
You're the jester of winter, no doubt or debate,
Tickling our senses, it's never too late!

The Secrets Behind the Frosted Pane

Oh, what tales you hold in your crystalline guise,
A universe frozen beneath playful skies.
Why am I wasting my warm cup of tea,
When you're here pulling pranks, just wait and see?

You sit there like art, a painter's cruel joke,
Each swirl and each twirl, just adds to the smoke.
Do you giggle at me from your chilly domain?
Scheming up mishaps with no hint of pain?

You've framed the world in a glistening sneeze,
As if nature coughed, but it aimed to please.
I peek through your patterns, my breath fogs the view,
Sending up bubbles for each giggle you brew.

Oh, how I ponder the laughs that you hide,
The whimsical wonders that live inside.
Your secrets unfold with each sunrise bright,
Transforming my morning into a comic delight!

When Nature Breathes in Silver

Nature sighs softly, with frosty delight,
Breathing out silver, painting all white.
The trees crack a smile, they wiggle with cheer,
Wearing coats made of shimmer, as winter draws near.

With every exhale, the world starts to freeze,
Nature's cold chuckle rustles the leaves.
I tiptoe outside, on a glistening floor,
Slipping and sliding, can't help but implore!

Your icy embrace makes the puddles squeak,
I tumble and roll, oh the joy of the week!
You whisper your giggles through branches so bare,
Promising mischief is hidden somewhere.

So here we all gather, endeavors so bold,
Warmed by laughter, as the winter unfolds.
Nature's a prankster, nervously clear,
With each chilly breath, we chuckle and cheer!

Veiled Realities of the Wintry World

Behind this glass veil, a jester resides,
Drawing doodles in white, oh how it hides!
It shakes up my senses, with each chilly breeze,
Turning mundane mornings into whimsical tease.

What are you whispering, you frosty old friend?
Pranking the sun, hoping it'll bend?
Do you hope that I'll slip when I step in your charms,
As you cape the world with your icy soft arms?

A world turned to giggles, a fusion of stars,
Where each glimmer hopes to be seen from afar.
You wrap up the rooftops, you blanket the lane,
Promising chuckles when we step out again.

So here's to your antics, you chilly delight,
You lace up our days with your sparkling light.
With every breath taken, I'm caught in your spell,
Laughter erupts, oh, we love you so well!

Luminous Patterns of the Wintry World

In the morning light, a glimpse we find,
A mural of chaos, by nature designed,
Little curls and swirls, oh what a sight,
Like a painter's doodle, bold and bright.

On our chilly glass, the sketches dance,
A rabbit or two, caught in a trance,
And look, there's a cat with a frosty beard,
Who knew winter had humor, so weird!

Sipping warm cocoa, we chuckle with glee,
At the art that the cold has left for free,
Each breath a fog, like a secret shared,
With whispers of mischief, winter's declared.

So let's celebrate this cheeky display,
Of nature's odd humor, come what may,
With a giggle and grin, we enjoy the show,
Luminous patterns, in cold's gentle glow.

The Silent Dance of Winter's Hand

A tap-tap-tapping on glass so smooth,
Winter's signature, in a playful groove,
With each little chill, it begins to twirl,
Turning mundane moments into a whirl.

Look closely now, what shapes we see,
A frosty hat on a table and three,
A snowman rising with a mischievous grin,
As if laughing at us from deep within.

The world outside, an ice cream parade,
With sprinkles of snowflakes, a lovely cascade,
And hot cocoa cups, perfectly aligned,
Passing warm giggles, generosity defined.

Oh chilly season, you're quite the prankster,
Turning our lives into a frosty jester,
We dance in the humor, wild and free,
In this silent waltz, just winter and me.

Celestial Frost, A Silent Muse

Stars twinkle bright on an icy sheet,
Each one a wink, a mischievous feat,
Crafting a comedy on wintry nights,
Who knew the cold could cook up delights?

Glancing outside, with noses all red,
We trace little figures in white, instead,
There's a dog doing yoga, in lopsided poses,
And a fish in a hat, oh how it dozes!

Our trousers are damp, but hearts are still light,
In puffy jackets, nothing can bite,
With laughter and warmth, we cherish this time,
Where the chill mixes laughter like a sweet rhyme.

So raise a toast to the chill in the air,
For humor in winter is beyond compare,
In celestial art, our dreams take flight,
As we embrace the laughter, in frosty delight.

Ghostly Whispers on Soft Canvas

The windows murmur, a secret they keep,
Giggling as shadows begin to creep,
With every little frostbite that clings,
A ghostly ballet, where laughter springs.

Look! There's a ghost with a top hat and cane,
Tango-ing with snowflakes, it's quite the scene,
And a waltzing snowman, who ricochets round,
In a snowy rave, without making a sound.

The giggles abound, as we peer through the glass,
At playful phantoms that come and then pass,
Whispers and chuckles float through the night,
Embracing the humor in frosty delight.

So let's join the party, in mittens and hats,
With giggles and warmth from our furry chitchats,
In this canvas of cool, so whimsically drawn,
We dance with the spirits, till the break of dawn.

The Art of Winter's Touch

A dance of white on glassy walls,
The artwork made when winter calls.
I'd sell my socks for a warm embrace,
But here I am, in this chilly space.

My breath makes clouds, a ghostly game,
I laugh at it, a puff of fame.
The patterns swirl, they twist and turn,
It's nature's way that makes me yearn.

I tap a tune on icy sheets,
A symphony of frosty beats.
The world outside, a frozen show,
Yet in here, I'm all aglow.

Through playful tricks, the sun peeks in,
Creating sparkles, a wintry grin.
I sip my cocoa, give a cheer,
For silly seasons, oh dear, oh dear!

Charmed by the Elemental Glow

I woke today to art sublime,
Nature's doodles, what a crime!
Each squiggle shines, a fancy touch,
But those drafts, they chill too much.

The kettle's on, I chase the warmth,
While outside swirls in crazy forms.
A snail once dressed in ice and flair,
I swear I saw it stop and stare!

The morning light, it winks and twirls,
At least my cup of joy unfurls.
I giggle hard at the cold's charade,
A jester in a snowy braid.

I join the scene and play along,
In jabberjays, we sing a song.
The laughs ring out, a bright cacophony,
Winter's grip can't dampen our symphony!

Glacial Secrets Against the Light

The sunlit shards, they gleam and glint,
Like diamonds spilled, oh what a hint!
But what's a snowman, in disguise?
Just a chilly guy with frosty eyes.

Through icy whispers, secrets tease,
I find a grin in every freeze.
The trees are dressed in icy wear,
While squirrels dart with frosty flair.

A sleepy bench, it creaks and sighs,
A seat for snowflakes, what a prize!
I'm sure I saw a penguin slide,
But it was just my dog outside!

Commerce thaws with laughter's might,
As jests are tossed, a silly fight.
Against the chill, we joke and jest,
A party wraps us in its vest!

Frosted Filigree of the Soul

On glass, a lace of winter's scheme,
A charming twist in every dream.
The chill that wraps, a funny coat,
While warm thoughts keep my heart afloat.

Shivering trees make silly poses,
In this glee, my spirit dozes.
With each breath, I breathe in cheer,
Winter's clasp, I hold it dear.

Through twinkling glances, I start to play,
With cheeky snowflakes that drift and sway.
The world may freeze, but here I laugh,
At all the winter's funny craft.

So toast to warmth, let spirits soar,
For chuckles light the icy floor.
In filigree, my heart is whole,
A winter's jest, a merry soul!

Chill Kisses on Glass

Tiny crystals dance and play,
They giggle on the glass today.
A chilly breath, a cheeky tease,
Turning warmth to winter's freeze.

Wipe it clear, oh what a scene,
A hidden face where laughs convene.
A frosty friend, it seems to say,
Let's play tricks in a snappy way!

Each little flake a witty jest,
Cozy blankets feel the best.
We sip our cocoa, watch them glint,
As chilly whispers leave a hint!

Through the panes, we spot the show,
Silly patterns tell us so.
Like children drawing in the snow,
What's next? Oh, who could ever know!

Whispers of Winter's Breath

A breath of chill, a playful tease,
A winter's whisper gives us freeze.
Each swirling edge, a joke well-made,
In crystal forms our laughter's played.

Look closely now, what's peeking through?
A snowflake smiles, just me and you.
Shadows dance in uneven light,
While penguins slide in sheer delight!

The window's dressed in ice-sleek gowns,
Yet warms our hearts, erasing frowns.
Each breath we see, a curious trick,
Like winter's magic, bold and quick!

Let's catch a chill, our giggles soar,
In frosty art, let's laugh some more.
Together we'll sip reality's cream,
And chase away the winter dream.

Crystal Lace of a Frozen Dawn

Morning light is pastel bright,
While crystal lace glitters in sight.
Windows adorned in a cheeky style,
Nature's artwork makes us smile.

Every stroke, a laughter traced,
A chilly hug, a harmless haste.
Join the fun, with a scratch and swipe,
Revealing art with every type!

Oh, can you see that cheeky swan?
With quirky wings at the break of dawn?
It wiggles, twirls, in a glassy dance,
Inviting us all to join the prance!

So here's to dawn with sparkle and glee,
Where wintry jokes are wild and free.
Let's hold our hot cups and gaze in awe,
At lacey jokes that winter saw.

The Quiet Embrace of December

December's chill brings quite a show,
Where warm hearts laugh, but windows grow.
A silent giggle, a frozen smile,
Bringing warmth in style and while.

Each chilly breath, an icy wink,
Makes us ponder, stop and think.
With hugs of warmth and laughter loud,
We dance like snowflakes, feeling proud!

Under blankets, we find our cheer,
While windows grin, hatching a sneer.
A breathy puff, a jolly tease,
Brings stories forth, like winter breeze!

So let's embrace this frosty time,
With silly thoughts and laughter's rhyme.
In winter's fold, we warm our hearts,
Amidst the chill, where fun imparts.

9 789916 945933